STAN LEE presents

the FANTASTIC FOUR®

A KANGAROO BOOK
PUBLISHED BY POCKET BOOKS NEW YORK

Marvel Comics'
THE FANTASTIC FOUR
POCKET BOOK edition published November, 1977
Second POCKET BOOK edition

This original POCKET BOOK edition is printed from
brand-new plates.
POCKET BOOK editions are published by
POCKET BOOKS,
a Simon & Schuster Division of
GULF & WESTERN CORPORATION
1230 Avenue of the Americas,
New York, N.Y. 10020.
Trademarks registered in the United States
and other countries.

A GALLERY OF THE

FANTASTIC FOUR'S

MIGHTIEST FOES!

THE MERCILESS MOLE MAN!

★

THE SKRULLS FROM OUTER SPACE!

★

THE MENACE OF THE MIRACLE MAN!

★

THE BIZARRE SUB-MARINER!

★

THE VENGEANCE OF DOCTOR DOOM!

★

THE DEADLY DUO!

★

LET THE VILLAINS
OF THE WORLD BEWARE!

PROLOGUE

They were the first! There had never been a team of superheroes like the FANTASTIC FOUR! They broke all the rules, shattered all the previous notions of how the "good guys" are supposed to behave when fighting the "bad guys," and—most important of all—they ushered us into the era of the "realistic fantasy" tale!

Okay, let's talk about it. What *were* the rules they broke? Well, first of all, who ever heard of a superhero team where the members would frequently fight amongst themselves? Who ever heard of costumed do-gooders who didn't have secret identities, who had to worry about meeting the rent payments for their skyscraper head-quarters, and who encountered almost as many defeats as victories in their offbeat careers? And, until the slightly sensational advent of the fabulous FANTASTIC FOUR, who ever heard of comic-book stories that continued from issue to issue, like a costumed version of a tv soap opera series?

Even the love interest violated all the precedents. The heroine wasn't coyly in love with the superhero while being totally and eternally unaware of his true identity. Heck no! Sue Storm was actually *engaged* to the garrulous Reed Richards—and she knew from the start that her rubbery-limbed Romeo was also the re-doubtable Mr. Fantastic! As for the seemingly obligatory teenager, youthful Johnny Storm was every bit as loud, pesty, and generally obnoxious as any titanically typical teenager of today.

5

In the case of Ben Grimm, it would take a book many times the size of this one to really do him justice. Suffice it to say that the ever-lovin' Thing is bad-tempered, ill-mannered, crude, and not the most attractive guy you're apt to meet. Therefore, what could be more natural than that he would turn out to be the FF's most popular and beloved member!

And finally, we come to the matter of the "realistic fantasy" tale. Perhaps this is what the Marvel group of comicbooks is most noted for—the combination of down-to-earth characterizations mingled with far-out story lines which are infinitely bigger than life—and it was the FANTASTIC FOUR which started the whole thing. Basically, the premise was a simple one. Let's face the fact that our stories are wildly imaginative, involving outer space, inner space, all four dimensions—with dozens of others tossed in—countless alien worlds and galaxies, monsters and demons and magicians and giants—and that's just scratching the surface! Now then, what if such fanciful, overblown story elements could be combined with real-life characters, locales, and situations? In other words, we try to take a concept as outlandish as a fairy tale and present it so realistically that it might be happening to you!

There you have the formula of the FANTASTIC FOUR, in a nutshell. And, even more than that, you have the start of the first series of FF epics, conveniently arranged in chronological order so that you can read them just as they were originally presented, almost two decades ago, when they ushered in the dawn of the now-famous Marvel Age of Comics. Comics have changed since FANTASTIC FOUR #1—styles of story and art have been continually evolving and improving. But, they were the first. And we rather hope, when you finish savoring the pages that lie ahead, that you'll contentedly murmur "—And they were the best!"

Excelsior!

Stan Lee

New York 1977

7

| | DR. REED RICHARDS | BEN GRIMM | SUSAN STORM | JOHNNY STORM |

HERE THEY ARE...

Stan Lee + Jack Kirby

THE FANTASTIC FOUR!

WITH THE SUDDEN FURY OF A THUNDERBOLT, A FLARE IS SHOT INTO THE SKY OVER CENTRAL CITY! THREE AWESOME WORDS TAKE FORM AS IF BY MAGIC, AND A LEGEND IS BORN!!

LOOK! IN THE SKY-- WHAT IN BLAZES DOES IT **MEAN?**

I DUNNO, BUT THE CROWDS ARE GETTIN' **PANICKY!**

RUMORS ARE FLYIN' ABOUT AN ALIEN INVASION!

ABOVE ALL THE HUBBUB AND EXCITEMENT, ONE STRANGE FIGURE HOLDS A STILL-SMOKING FLARE GUN! ONE STRANGE MAN WHO IS SOMEHOW **MORE** THAN JUST A MAN--FOR HE IS THE LEADER OF... THE FANTASTIC FOUR!

IT IS THE FIRST TIME I HAVE FOUND IT NECESSARY TO GIVE THE SIGNAL! I PRAY IT WILL BE THE **LAST!**

9

10

11

12

13

14

15

18

19

THE FANTASTIC FOUR MEET THE MOLE MAN!

BUT WE SHALL RETURN TO THE MOLEMAN BEFORE LONG! FIRST, LET US TURN OUR ATTENTION BACK TO THE FANTASTIC FOUR, AS THEY GAZE IN ASTONISHMENT AT DR. REED RICHARDS' SUPER-SENSITIVE RADARSCOPE...

THERE! IT HAS HAPPENED AGAIN! THIS TIME IN FRENCH EQUATORIAL AFRICA!

BUT HOW? WHY?

THAT'S WHAT WE'VE GOT TO FIND OUT!

BY STUDYING THE CAVE-INS CAREFULLY, I'VE PIN-POINTED AN ISLAND LOCATED EXACTLY BETWEEN THEM! THAT IS WHERE WE WILL FIND OUR ANSWER! IT IS KNOWN AS MONSTER ISLE!

MONSTER ISLE! THAT'S JUST A FAIRY TALE! THERE'S NO SUCH PLACE!

ONLY ONE WAY TO FIND OUT, BEN!

AND FIND OUT THEY DO! HOURS LATER, ABOARD THEIR SMALL, PRIVATE JET, THE FANTASTIC FOUR SEE A STRANGE MOUNTAIN RISING FROM THE SEA, LIKE AN UNEARTHLY GROTESQUE FACE!! THEY HAVE FOUND... MONSTER ISLE!

THERE IT IS!

LITTLE DREAMING WHAT AWAITS THEM, THEY CLIMB TO THE TOP OF THE FORBIDDING PEAK...

IF THIS IS JUST A WILD GOOSE CHASE, MISTER, I'LL MAKE SURE YOU LIVE TO REGRET IT!

SAVE YOUR BREATH FOR THE CLIMB, GRUE-SOME!

HOLD IT!! I HEAR SOMETHING!!

IT'S COMING FROM BELOW!

LOOK!! THOSE EYES...

SUDDENLY, A LIVING THREE-HEADED NIGHT-MARE HURLS ITSELF AT THEM FROM OVER THE EDGE OF THE PEAK OF MONSTER ISLE!

17

25

26

THE MOLEMAN'S SECRET!

BEFORE WE WITNESS THE BREATH-TAKING CONCLUSION OF OUR AMAZING TALE, LET US GATHER TOGETHER ALL THE LOOSE ENDS! LET US RETURN TO THE TWO MEMBERS OF THE FANTASTIC FOUR WHO DID NOT FALL BELOW DURING THE CAVE-IN...

REED... AND JOHNNY... GOT TO FIND THEM!!

WAIT! THAT NOISE -- BEHIND ME!! WHAT--??

BUT OTHER EARS ALSO HEAR THE MENACING SOUNDS... AND OTHER EYES BEHOLD THE FRIGHTENING SIGHT...

THE EYES OF... THE THING!!

DUCK, SUE! OUT OF THE WAY!

LET ME HANDLE 'IM!

20

THE SECOND GIGANTIC GUARDIAN OF MONSTER ISLE IS POWERFUL BEYOND BELIEF...BUT HE IS FIGHTING AN ENEMY WHOSE EVERY ATOM HAS BEEN CHARGED WITH COSMIC RAYS...AN ENEMY WHO **CAN'T BE STOPPED!**

YOU'VE DONE IT, BEN! YOU'VE BEATEN HIM!

WHAT DID YOU **EXPECT??**

I'M **THE THING**, AIN'T I??

NOW LET'S GO AND FIND THAT SKINNY, LOUD-MOUTHED BOY-FRIEND OF YOURS!

OH, BEN-- IF ONLY YOU COULD STOP HATING REED FOR WHAT HAPPENED TO YOU!

AND WHAT OF REED RICHARDS? AND SUE'S BROTHER, JOHNNY? WE AGAIN DESCEND TO THE DEPTHS OF MONSTER ISLE WHERE WE FIND THEM CONFRONTED BY THE STRANGEST MENACE OF ALL TIME... THE MOLEMAN!

SO, YOU HAVE NEVER BEFORE **HEARD** OF THE MOLEMAN, EH? WELL, **SOON THE WORLD** SHALL HEAR OF ME!!

FOR SOON, THE MOLEMAN WILL HAVE THE ENTIRE WORLD IN HIS **POWER!**

HOW DID YOU **GET** HERE? WHAT **IS** THIS PLACE?

21

"IT ALL STARTED LONG AGO!! BECAUSE THE PEOPLE OF THE SURFACE WORLD MOCKED ME!"

WHAT? ME GO OUT WITH YOU? DON'T MAKE ME LAUGH!

I KNOW YOU'RE QUALIFIED, BUT YOU CAN'T WORK HERE! YOU'D SCARE OUR OTHER EMPLOYEES AWAY!

HEY, IS THAT YOUR FACE, OR ARE YOU WEARIN' A MASK? HAW HAW!

"FINALLY, I COULD STAND IT NO LONGER! I DECIDED TO STRIKE OUT ALONE...TO SEARCH FOR A NEW WORLD ...THE LEGENDARY LAND AT THE CENTER OF THE EARTH! A WORLD WHERE I COULD BE KING! MY TRAVELS TOOK ME ALL OVER THE GLOBE..."

EVEN THIS LONELINESS IS BETTER THAN THE CRUELTY OF MY FELLOW MEN!

"AND THEN, JUST WHEN I HAD ALMOST ABANDONED HOPE... WHEN MY LITTLE SKIFF HAD BEEN WASHED ASHORE HERE ON MONSTER ISLE, I FOUND IT!"

THAT STRANGE CAVERN! WHERE CAN IT LEAD TO?

"I SOON SAW WHERE IT LED... IT LED TO THE LAND OF MY DREAMS..."

DOWN THERE...BELOW-- I'VE FOUND IT!! IT'S EARTH'S CENTER!

"BUT IN THE DREAD SILENCE OF THAT HUGE CAVERN, THE SUDDEN SHOCK OF MY LOUD OUTCRY CAUSED A VIOLENT AVALANCHE, AND..."

"...WHEN IT WAS OVER, I HAD SOMEHOW MIRACULOUSLY SURVIVED THE FALL....BUT, DUE TO THE IMPACT OF THE CRASH, HAD LOST MOST OF MY SIGHT! YES, I HAD FOUND THE CENTER OF EARTH--BUT I WAS STRANDED HERE...LIKE A HUMAN MOLE!!"

22

THAT WAS TO BE THE LAST OF MY MISFORTUNES! MY LUCK BEGAN TO TURN IN MY FAVOR! I MASTERED THE CREATURES DOWN HERE-- MADE THEM DO MY BIDDING-- AND WITH THEIR HELP, I CARVED OUT AN UNDER-GROUND EMPIRE!

A NOTE OF MADNESS CREEPS INTO THE MOLE'S VOICE AS HE SPEAKS OF HIS POWER! AND THEN, HE MAKES HIS FIRST FATAL MISTAKE...

I CONQUERED EVERYTHING ABOUT ME! I EVEN LEARNED TO SENSE THINGS IN THE DARK-- LIKE A MOLE! HERE, I'LL **SHOW** YOU! TRY TO STRIKE ME WITH THAT POLE! **TRY** IT, I SAY!!

HAH! I SENSED THAT BLOW COMING! NOTHING CAN TAKE ME BY SURPRISE! AND, I HAVE DEVELOPED **OTHER** SENSES TOO, LIKE THOSE OF THE BAT--

I POSSESS A NATURAL RADAR SENSE... A WARNING SYSTEM WHICH ENABLES ME TO EVADE DANGER WHATEVER STRIKES AT ME!

COMPARED TO THE MOLE-MAN, YOU ARE SLOW, CLUMSY!! HAH HAH!!

SEE HOW EASILY I DEFEAT YOU... OR ANY OTHERS WHO TRY TO DEFY ME!

NOW, BEFORE I SLAY YOU ALL, BEHOLD MY MASTER PLAN! SEE THIS MAP OF MY UNDERGROUND EMPIRE! EACH TUNNEL LEADS TO A MAJOR CITY! AS SOON AS I HAVE WRECKED EVERY ATOMIC PLANT, EVERY SOURCE OF EARTHLY POWER, MY MIGHTY MOLE CREATURES WILL ATTACK AND DESTROY EVERYTHING THAT LIVES ABOVE THE SURFACE!

AND NOW, AT MY SIGNAL, THOSE CREATURES OF DARKNESS, MY DENIZENS OF EARTH'S CENTER, SHALL DISPOSE OF ALL OF YOU WITLESS INTRUDERS!

WE'LL **SEE** ABOUT THAT, MOLE!!

THE THING!!

MOVING LIKE A WELL-OILED FIGHTING MACHINE, THE FANTASTIC FOUR, WITH THE DEADLY MOLEMAN IN THEIR GRASP, RACE FOR THE SURFACE... BUT THEN THEIR EVIL ANTAGONIST SEIZES THE SIGNAL CORD AGAIN, AND,..

YOU HAVEN'T WON YET! EVEN YOU CAN'T DEFEAT ALL OF MY UNDER-EARTH HORDE!

HURRY, REED... HURRY!

CAN'T YOU EVEN HOLD ON TO ONE LITTLE GUY?

AND THEN THEY COME... LIKE FIGMENTS OF A MAD NIGHTMARE... ROARING, RUNNING, SNARLING... THE MOLEMAN'S ENTIRE ARMY OF UNDERGROUND GARGOYLES!!

BUT THEY HADN'T COUNTED ON THE UNBELIEVABLE POWER OF THE HUMAN TORCH! FLYING BETWEEN HIS FANTASTIC ALLIES, AND THE PURSUING HORDE, HE BLAZES A FIERY SWATH WHICH MELTS THE SOFT EARTH...

THIS WILL CAUSE A ROCKSLIDE, SEALING US OFF FROM THOSE CREATURES!

WE DID IT...WE'RE FREE!! AND THE ENTRANCE TO THE MOLEMAN'S EMPIRE IS SEALED FOREVER!

MOMENTS LATER...

BUT WHERE IS THE MOLEMAN?

I LEFT HIM BEHIND--HE'LL NEVER TROUBLE ANYONE AGAIN!

AND THE WORDS OF MR. FANTASTIC ARE INDEED PROPHETIC... AS, SECONDS LATER...

HE'S DESTROYED THE ENTIRE ISLE! HE'S SEALED HIMSELF BELOW--FOREVER!

IT'S BEST THAT WAY! THERE WAS NO PLACE FOR HIM IN OUR WORLD ...PERHAPS HE'LL FIND PEACE DOWN THERE... I HOPE SO!

I JUST HOPE WE HAVE SEEN THE LAST OF HIM!

BUT, WHETHER WE'VE SEEN THE LAST OF THE MOLEMAN OR NOT, WE WILL SEE MUCH MORE OF THE MOST AMAZING QUARTET IN HISTORY, IN THE NEXT GREAT ISSUE OF-- THE FANTASTIC FOUR! DON'T MISS IT!!

THE END

33

THE FANTASTIC FOUR

MEET THE SKRULLS FROM OUTER SPACE!

WHAT IS HAPPENING HERE?? WHAT IS *THE THING* DOING, SWIMMING MILES OFF-SHORE TOWARDS A LONELY TEXAS TOWER? WHY DO HIS EYES GLEAM WITH A SINISTER, CRAFTY LIGHT? SILENTLY, POWER-FULLY, HE SWIMS CLOSER-- CLOSER--HIDDEN BY THE DEEPENING TWILIGHT.'

UNSEEN, UNSUSPECTED, HE SWIMS TOWARDS ONE OF THE TOWER'S MIGHTY SUPPORT POSTS...

AND THEN...

LIKE A FALLEN GIANT, THE MIGHTY STRUCTURE CRUMBLES AND SLOWLY SINKS INTO THE SEA!

THE BOATS! GET TO THE BOATS!

LUCKY WE ALL GOT AWAY WITH OUR LIVES!

BUT WHAT *CAUSED* IT? WAS IT A DEPTH CHARGE?

LOOK! SWIMMING AWAY! IT...IT'S *THE THING!* HE DID IT! THE THING WRECKED THE TOWER!

MEANWHILE, MANY MILES AWAY, IN ONE OF AMERICA'S MOST EXPENSIVE JEWELRY STORES...

WE DON'T USUALLY TAKE THIS GEM OUT OF THE VAULT TO SHOW PEOPLE, MISS STORM! IT'S WORTH ALMOST TEN MILLION DOLLARS! BUT FOR *YOU,* I CAN MAKE AN EXCEPTION!

YES, IT IS JUST WHAT I'VE BEEN LOOKING FOR!

IT-- IT *IS?*

I MUST ADMIT I NEVER REALLY EXPECTED ANYONE TO *BUY* SUCH AN EXPENSIVE GEM!

BUY?

I DON'T INTEND TO BUY IT!

SHE--SHE'S *GONE!* GUARDS! GUARDS!!

WE HAVE DONE OUR WORK WELL! WE HAVE *SUCCEEDED!*

YES! BY NOW THE ENTIRE NATION IS HUNTING THE FANTASTIC FOUR!

THE ORDER IS OUT-- SHOOT ON SIGHT! THERE WILL BE NO PLACE TO HIDE!

I'VE BEEN WONDERING --HOW DID YOU ALL ACCOMPLISH YOUR FEATS?

ALTHOUGH THE ARMY THINKS IT WAS DONE BY BRUTE STRENGTH, I SECRETLY DEMOLISHED THE WATER TOWER BY MEANS OF THIS CONCEALED ELECTRONIC DETONATOR!

AS FOR ME, I QUICKLY CHANGED MY SIZE TO ONLY A FEW INCHES TALL-- BUT EVERYONE *THOUGHT* I HAD BECOME INVISIBLE!

MY TASK WAS AN EASY ONE! WITH THIS POWERED ANTI-GRAVITY GEAR AND A LOW VELOCITY THERMAL BOMB, I REALLY SEEMED TO BE A FLYING, FLAMING HUMAN!

AS FOR *ME,* I NEEDED NO SPECIAL DEVICES! FOR IT'S AN EASY MATTER FOR ME TO ALTER MY BODY IN ANY WAY I DESIRE!

JUST AS IT IS EASY FOR *ALL* OF US TO DO SO!

WHICH IS WHY THE UNSUSPECTING EARTHMEN WILL NEVER KNOW THAT WE *SKRULLS* HAVE *IMPERSONATED* THEIR FAMOUS FANTASTIC ENEMIES!

NOW, ALL THAT REMAINS IS FOR THE EARTHLINGS *THEMSELVES* TO HUNT DOWN AND DESTROY THE FANTASTIC FOUR!

AND ONCE THE FANTASTIC FOUR ARE SLAIN, NO POWER ON EARTH CAN STOP THE SKRULL INVASION!

EVEN NOW, OUR MOTHER SHIP HOVERS UNSEEN, ABOVE EARTH'S ATMOSPHERE, WAITING FOR OUR SIGNAL TO LAUNCH THE ATTACK!

AND THUS WE LEARN THE SECRETS OF THE INCREDIBLE FEATS WE HAVE SEEN! ABOVE US, *THE SKRULLS FROM OUTER SPACE* HAVE TURNED ALL EARTH AGAINST THE FANTASTIC FOUR!

DAILY GLOBE
FANTASTIC FOUR DECLARED PUBLIC ENEMIES
HUNT WIDENS FOR MEMBERS OF STRANGE GROUP...

THE FANT FOUR MU...

DAILY BUGLE
DRAGNET OUT FOR FANTASTIC FOUR!

SHOOT TO KILL!

4!

WHILE MILES AWAY, IN AN ISOLATED HUNTING LODGE, THE MOST UNUSUAL HUMANS ON EARTH LEARN WHAT HAS HAPPENED...

...THE FANTASTIC FOUR HAVE BECOME THE MOST DANGEROUS MENACE WE HAVE EVER FACED! THEY MUST BE FOUND! THEY MUST BE PUNISHED!

TURN THAT RADIO OFF! WE HAVE TO THINK!

IT IS OBVIOUS THAT SOME FOURSOME IS IMPERSONATING US! BUT HOW? WHY?

BUT, REED, HOW COULD ANY HUMANS IMPERSONATE US? NO ONE ELSE HAS OUR POWERS!

AW, I'M NOT WORRIED! REED WILL FIGURE OUT WHAT TO DO, AND THEN WE'LL TAKE CARE OF THEM, I'LL BET!

BAH! WHILE THE THREE OF YOU BEAT YOUR GUMS, THE WHOLE COUNTRY IS HUNTING US AS THOUGH WE'RE FOUR MONSTERS!

WELL, MAYBE THEY'RE RIGHT! MAYBE I AM A MONSTER! I LOOK LIKE ONE -- AND SOMETIMES I FEEL LIKE ONE!

BUT NOBODY'S CATCHIN' ME WITHOUT A FIGHT! IF THEY SAY I'M A MENACE, I'LL BE A MENACE! I'LL SHOW 'EM ALL!

THAT'S WHAT I'LL DO TO ANYONE WHO GETS IN MY WAY!

REED! STOP HIM! HE'S GOING MAD!

CRASH!

EASY, THING, EASY! WE CAN'T FIGHT THE WHOLE HUMAN RACE!

FIRST, WE'VE GOT TO FIND OUT WHAT'S BEHIND THIS PLAN TO DISCREDIT US!

TALK! *TALK!* ALL YOU EVER DO IS TALK! BUT I'M NOT *BUILT* THAT WAY! I WANT ACTION!

I *KNOW* YOU DO, THING! BUT WE CAN'T FLY OFF THE HANDLE! WE'VE GOT TO WAIT TILL WE KNOW WHO'S *BEHIND* ALL THIS!

WAIT?? THAT'S ALL RIGHT FOR YOU, TORCH! AT LEAST YOU'RE *HUMAN!*

BUT HOW WOULD YOU LIKE TO BE ME? I WON'T WAIT ANY LONGER! I'M GOING OUT... ...TO *FIGHT!* ...TO *SMASH!*

REED, HOW MUCH MORE OF THIS CAN WE TAKE? SOONER OR LATER, THE THING WILL RUN AMOK AND NONE OF US WILL BE ABLE TO STOP HIM!

SHE'S RIGHT, REED! WE'VE GOT TO *DO* SOMETHING ABOUT HIM!

NO! WE MUST BE PATIENT! AFTER ALL, HE'S NOT REALLY TO BLAME! IT'S ACTUALLY *MY* FAULT THAT HE IS THE WAY HE IS!

"IT WAS *MY* FAULT THAT OUR FLIGHT TO MARS FAILED AND WE NEARLY LOST OUR LIVES WHEN WE CRASH-LANDED ON EARTH!...

"IT WAS MY FAULT THAT THE COSMIC RAYS OF SPACE TURNED SUE INTO A SOMETIMES INVISIBLE GIRL!...

"...THE SAME RAYS WHICH MADE A POWERFUL, BRUTAL THING OUT OF POOR *BEN!* ...

"IT WAS BECAUSE OF MY OVERSIGHT THAT JOHNNY WAS TRANSFORMED INTO A TEMPORARY HUMAN TORCH BY THOSE FANTASTIC RAYS!...

"WHILE THE COMPOSITION OF MY OWN BODY ATOMS HAS BEEN SO CHANGED THAT I CAN STRETCH AND CHANGE MYSELF INTO ALMOST ANY CONCEIVABLE SHAPE!"

I CAN'T PUNISH THE THING WHEN THE FAULT IS *MINE!*

OKAY, FORGET *HIM!* WHAT DO WE DO *NOW?*

39

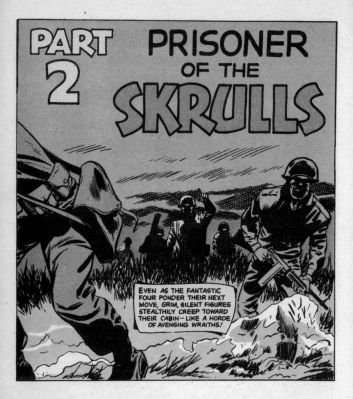

41

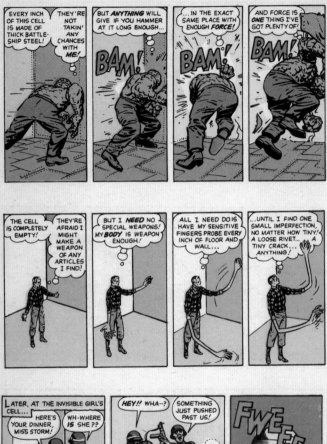

43

45

46

47

50

51

52

53

THERE GOES THE *THIRD* ONE!

IT-- IT'S *UNBELIEVABLE* HOW THEY CAN CHANGE THEIR FORMS AT WILL!

GOTCHA!

MOMENTS LATER, AFTER THE THREE SKRULLS HAVE CHANGED BACK TO THEIR NORMAL FORMS...

WELL, CHIEF-- WHAT HAVE YOU TO SAY FOR YOUR-SELF NOW?

LOOKS LIKE I MAY START BELIEVIN' IN *SANTA CLAUS*, TOO!

SO *THEY'RE* THE CHARACTERS WHO IMPERSONATED YOU FOUR AND COMMITTED THOSE CRIMES, EH?

THAT'S RIGHT!

THE FOURTH ONE IS ON HIS WAY TO ANOTHER GALAXY NOW WITH THE REST OF HIS INVASION FLEET!

IMAGINE! YOU FOUR FOILED AN INTER-PLANETARY INVASION, AND WE'VE BEEN HUNTING YOU LIKE CRIMINALS!

BUT WE *STILL* HAVE ONE BIG PROBLEM LEFT--

AND HOW!

WHAT'S THAT?

THAT, MY YOUNG, FIERY FRIEND, IS ... WHAT DO WE *DO* WITH THOSE THREE SKRULLS ??

IF WE PUT THEM IN PRISON, THEY'LL PROBABLY TURN THEMSELVES INTO CATERPILLARS AND SLIP THROUGH THE BARS!

CHIEF, WILL YOU TRUST *US* TO SOLVE THE PROBLEM FOR YOU?

57

58

60

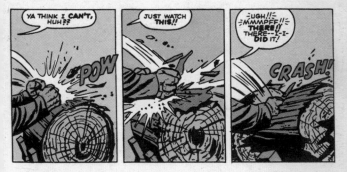

61

62

67

CHAPTER III "THE FLAME THAT DIED!"

THING!! LOOK!! IT'S THE TORCH!

HE'S FOUND THE MONSTER!

THAT MEANS ONE THING...

YEAH! THE MIRACLE MAN MUST BE THERE, TOO! LET'S GO!

YOU STAY HIDDEN, SUE, IN CASE WE NEED YOU!

AS FOR ME, I'M GETTIN' OUTTA THIS MONKEY SUIT SO I CAN MOVE!

70

71

CHAPTER IV "IN THE SHADOW OF DEFEAT!"

AN HOUR LATER...
WHY DID YOU LET SUE TACKLE THE MIRACLE MAN BY HER-SELF?

BECAUSE THAT'S THE WAY SHE WANTED IT, SQUIRT! NOW SHUDDUP AND LET US THINK!

SIMMER DOWN, THING! AND YOU TOO, TORCH! WHEN SUE SIGNALS US TO COME RUNNING, WE'VE GOT TO BE READY!

READY? I'M ALWAYS READY!! THE NEXT TIME I GET WITHIN GRABBING DISTANCE OF THAT GUY, I'LL MAKE MINCEMEAT OF HIM!

HE THINKS HIS POWERS ARE GREATER THAN OURS, HUH? WELL, THEY AIN'T! HE'S JUST TRICKIER, THAT'S ALL!! NOTHING'S MORE POWERFUL THAN THOSE COSMIC RAYS THAT TURNED US INTO WHAT WE ARE!

"I'LL NEVER BURN THE MEMORY OF THAT ACCURSED DAY FROM MY MIND..."

"THE FLIGHT INTO SPACE - THE BOMBARD-MENT OF THE COSMIC RAYS, AND THEN... THE CRASH!"

73

74

75

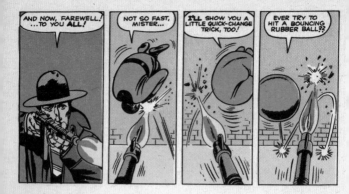

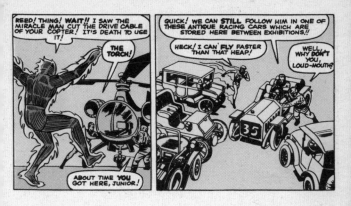

79

HE IS NO MIRACLE MAN! HE HAS NO MAGIC POWERS! HE IS MERELY A CLEVER HYPNOTIST, A MASTER OF MASS ILLUSION! THE MONSTER NEVER *REALLY* MOVED--HE HYPNOTIZED US INTO *THINKING* IT DID!

HE DIDN'T REALLY SPLIT THAT LOG ON STAGE WITH ONE FINGER!...HE MADE EVERYONE *THINK* HE DID! AND THE SAME FOR *ALL* HIS SUPPOSEDLY MIRACULOUS FEATS!

HOW--HOW DID YOU GUESS?

BECAUSE A *TRUE* MIRACLE MAN WOULD NOT HAVE *NEEDED* TO STEAL JEWELS...HE COULD HAVE CONJURED UP ALL THE WEALTH IN THE WORLD! A MIRACLE MAN WOULD NOT HAVE NEEDED TO FLEE FROM US... YOU COULD HAVE SIMPLY VANISHED...OR CAUSED *US* TO DISAPPEAR, FOREVER!

BUT NOW, YOUR HYPNOTIC POWER IS GONE, DUE TO TORCH'S ALMOST BLINDING FLASH!

WAIT A MINUTE, REED!! ARE YOU TRYIN' TO GIVE THAT FLAMING JUVENILE DELINQUENT THE CREDIT FOR THIS CAPER??

OH, PLEASE! DON'T START ARGUING AMONG YOUR-SELVES AGAIN! I--I JUST CAN'T *STAND* ANY MORE!

RELAX, SIS! THEY'RE NOT GONNA ARGUE ABOUT *ME* ANY MORE! I HAD ALL THE BOSSIN' AROUND I CAN TAKE! I'M CUTTIN' OUT OF THIS COMBO, RIGHT *NOW!*

BUT YOU *CAN'T* QUIT US, JOHNNY!

AW, LET HIM *GO!* HE'S MORE TROUBLE THAN HE'S WORTH!

TORCH!! COME BACK! PLEASE!!

IT'S TOO LATE, SUE!

OH, REED, WHAT WILL BECOME OF HIM!

IT'S NOT *HIM* I'M WORRIED ABOUT...

...IT'S *MANKIND!* FOR WHAT WILL WE DO--

WHAT *CAN* WE DO, IF... IF HE SHOULD TURN *AGAINST* US?!!

NEXT ISSUE, THE SUSPENSE MOUNTS UNBEARABLY AS THE TORCH STRIKES BACK! AND DON'T BE SURPRISED TO SEE ANOTHER GREAT CHARACTER WHOM YOU DEMANDED WE BRING BACK! ALL IN THE NEXT WONDERFUL ISSUE!

23

THE END

81

THE FANTASTIC FOUR in THE COMING OF...
SUB-MARINER!

AT A SECRET SKYSCRAPER HIDEOUT, IN THE CAVERNS OF NEW YORK, THREE OF THE MOST FANTASTIC HUMANS ON EARTH ARE FOUND! BUT... WHERE IS THE *FOURTH*??

SOMEWHERE OUT THERE, AMONG THE TEEMING MILLIONS OF THE CITY, THE HUMAN TORCH IS HIDING FROM US!

AND WE'VE *GOT* TO FIND HIM!

Stan Lee + J. Kirby

BAH! FOR ALL I CARE, HE CAN STAY HIDDEN!

CHAPTER 1 "ON THE TRAIL of the TORCH!"

HE'S NOTHIN' BUT A SPOILED BRAT OF A TEEN-AGER! WHAT DO WE NEED HIM FOR?

HOW CAN YOU TALK ABOUT MY *BROTHER* THAT WAY? HE MAY BE HURT, OR IN TROUBLE!

DON'T WORRY ABOUT THE TORCH, SUE! I'M *SURE* HE'S OKAY!

AS FOR YOU, THING, IT'S *YOUR* FAULT THAT HE RAN OFF!

SURE! SURE! EVERYTHING AROUND HERE IS MY FAULT!

84

I'VE GOTTA DO A LITTLE WELDING BEFORE I CAN FIX THOSE GASKETS!

SO, HERE GOES!

FLAME ON!

HEY, GANG! DIG THAT!

THIS BEATS A WELDING IRON ANY DAY!

AND IF THERE'S A REAL BIG WELDING JOB TO DO...

NOTICE HOW I CAN CONTROL MY FLAME? BY NOT MOVING, IT DOESN'T GO NEAR THE GASOLINE!

BUT, AT THAT VERY MOMENT, OUTSIDE THE GARAGE...

BEFORE I KNOCK MYSELF OUT SEARCHING THE WHOLE CITY, I'LL PLAY A HUNCH!

THAT BRAT USED TO HANG AROUND HERE, FIDDLIN' WITH HOT RODS, EVERY CHANCE HE GOT!

HEY!! I CAN FEEL THE HEAT! HE'S INSIDE!

THE THING!!

YOU'RE BLAMED RIGHT IT'S THE THING, TORCH!! AND NOW I'LL TEACH YOU WHAT HAPPENS TO DESERTERS!

AND YOUR FLAME DOESN'T SCARE ME NOW! I KNOW YOU CAN'T MOVE WHILE YOU'RE BURNING, BECAUSE THERE'S GASOLINE ALL OVER HERE! ONE SPARK AND YOUR PALS ARE DONE FOR!

5

CHAPTER 2

ENTER THE SUB-MARINER!

AS THE THING SINKS TO HIS KNEES IN HELPLESS RAGE, JOHNNY STORM REACHES THE OUTSKIRTS OF-- THE BOWERY!

THIS IS ONE PLACE WHERE NOBODY'LL FIND ME! I'LL JUST LOSE MYSELF AMONG ALL THE OTHER HUMAN DERELICTS HERE!

SAM'S MARKET

MIGHT AS WELL FIND A PLACE TO SACK DOWN FOR THE NIGHT! I GUESS THIS ONE IS NO WORSE THAN THE OTHERS!

MEIG HOTEL 25¢

A FEW MINUTES LATER...

WELL, IT'S NOT THE WALDORF, BUT IT'LL KEEP ME SAFELY HIDDEN WHILE I PLAN MY NEXT MOVE!

RULES

SAY! LOOK AT THIS OLD, BEAT-UP COMIC MAG! IT'S FROM THE 1940's!!

THE SUB-MARINER!!

SUB-MARINER

I REMEMBER SIS TALKING ABOUT HIM ONCE! HE USED TO BE THE WORLD'S MOST UNUSUAL CHARACTER!

YEAH, JUST LIKE SIS SAID, HE COULD LIVE UNDERWATER, AND WAS AS STRONG AS TEN MEN!

I WONDER WHAT EVER HAPPENED TO HIM? HE WAS SUPPOSED TO BE IMMORTAL!

READIN' ABOUT SUB-MARINER, HUM?

WE GOT A STUMBLE-BUM RIGHT HERE WHO'S AS STRONG AS THAT JOKER WAS SUPPOSED TO BE!

HEY, OLD MAN-- WAKE UP!

YOU WOULDN'T THINK IT TO LOOK AT THAT OLD BUM, BUT JUST WAIT!

HUH?! WHAT--?

90

91

92

CHAPTER 3

LET THE WORLD BEWARE!

SUE STORM, TOO, PROWLS THE VAST METROPOLIS IN HER OTHER IDENTITY AS *THE INVISIBLE GIRL!*

THE BOWERY! HAVEN OF LOST SOULS!

I CAN'T BELIEVE THAT JOHNNY WOULD EVER COME *HERE!*

C'MON, PAL! IF YOU *ARE* THE SUB-MARINER, I KNOW THE *ONE* THING THAT'LL BRING BACK YOUR MEMORY!

NO, I'M WASTING MY TIME HERE! I'LL GO AND SEARCH SOME *OTHER* PART OF TOWN!

THUS DOES DESTINY TOY WITH THE LIVES OF HUMANS! AND SO, UNWITTINGLY, THE INVISIBLE GIRL WALKS AWAY FROM THE VERY ONE SHE SEEKS!

OKAY, THE COAST IS CLEAR...

FLAME ON!

RELAX, MISTER! I'M NOT GONNA DROP YOU! NOT TILL WE COME TO...

...*THE SEA!*

IF HE *IS* THE SUB-MARINER, THE WATER WILL BRING BACK HIS MEMORY AND HIS FULL POWERS! IF NOT, I'LL DIVE IN AND SAVE HIM!

ONCE SUBMERGED IN THE MIGHTY SEA, A STARTLING CHANGE COMES OVER THE STRANGE DERELICT! IN ONE SWEEPING MOTION, HE HURLS HIS OUTER GARMENTS FROM HIM...

AND STANDS REVEALED AS THE LEGENDARY PRINCE OF THE SEA... THE INVINCIBLE *NAMOR, THE SUB-MARINER!!*

I *REMEMBER* NOW!! I *AM* THE SUB-MARINER! MY FAMILY--- MY FRIENDS! MY UNDERSEA KINGDOM... I MUST RETURN!...

TRAVELLING IN HIS NATIVE ELEMENT LIKE A CAREENING TORPEDO, PRINCE NAMOR SOON REACHES HIS ALMOST-FORGOTTEN LAND, ONLY TO FIND...

DESTROYED!! IT'S ALL DESTROYED!!

THAT GLOW IN THE WATER-- IT'S *RADIOACTIVITY!!* NOW I KNOW WHAT HAPPENED!!

THE *HUMANS* DID IT, UNTHINKINGLY, WITH THEIR *ACCURSED ATOMIC TESTS!*

MY PEOPLE COULD NOT BE HARMED BY RADIATION, BUT WHEN THEIR HOMES WERE DESTROYED, THEY MUST HAVE GONE *ELSEWHERE!* THE OCEANS ARE *VAST, ENDLESS!* HOW SHALL I EVER *FIND* THEM?

MINUTES LATER...

BUT THE HUMANS SHALL *PAY* FOR THIS! I *SWEAR* IT!!

HE'S *BACK!!*

YOU YOUNG *FOOL!!* DO NOT FEEL *PROUD* OF WHAT YOU HAVE DONE!!

FOR, BY RETURNING MY MEMORY, YOU HAVE SIGNED THE *DEATH WARRANT* OF THE HUMAN RACE!

WHA--? WHAT ARE YOU *TALKING* ABOUT?

REVENGE!! I'M TALKING ABOUT THE REVENGE I SHALL HAVE FOR THE DESTRUCTION OF MY UNDERSEA KINGDOM!!

I AM THE *MIGHTIEST* LIVING MORTAL ON EARTH!!

AND NOW, MANKIND SHALL *FEEL* THAT MIGHT... AS IT IS TURNED *AGAINST* YOU ALL!

97

HEARING THE EERIE, UNDERSEA BLAST, WITH ONE EARTH-SHAKING SHRUG, THE UNDERSEA BEHEMOTH SHAKES OFF THE SLEEP OF AGES, AND...

I'VE *DONE* IT! I'VE AWAKENED THE MONSTER! NOW *NOTHING* CAN STOP HIM!

HE'LL FOLLOW THE TRUMPET-HORN WHEREVER IT LEADS...

AND, IN THE HANDS OF SUB-MARINER, IT LEADS TO -- *THE SURFACE WORLD!*

FOR THE LOVE OF HEAVEN... *LOOK!!*

MINDLESSLY, THE GIGANTIC CREATURE SPLINTERS THE OLD TRAMP STEAMER, AS THE CREW ESCAPES TO SOUND THE ALARM...

WE--WE ARE TOO *SMALL* FOR HIM TO NOTICE!

I'VE GOT THE EMERGENCY RADIO WORKING, SIR!

AND, WITHIN SECONDS...

I *KNOW* IT SOUNDS IMPOSSIBLE, BUT...

NOWADAYS, *NOTHING* IS IMPOSSIBLE!

THEY SAID IT'S HEADED TOWARDS NEW YORK!

FOR THE FIRST TIME IN HISTORY, THE INCREDIBLE ORDER IS GIVEN... *EVACUATE NEW YORK!*

DON'T PANIC!! JUST KEEP MOVING!

HURRY! HURRY!

AND, THRU THE NOW-SILENT CANYONS OF THE DESERTED CITY, THE NATION'S MOST POWERFUL WEAPONS ARE BROUGHT INTO POSITION!

HERE IT COMES!

99

104

THE FANTASTIC FOUR, IN...
"PRISONERS OF DOCTOR DOOM!"

THE FANTASTIC FOUR!! HAH! LITTLE DO THEY DREAM THEY ARE NAUGHT BUT *PAWNS* IN THE HANDS OF DOCTOR DOOM!

DEMONS

PART 1

Stan Lee + J. KIRBY

SCIENCE AND SORCERY

BUT NOW IT IS TIME TO LET THE FANTASTIC FOUR FEEL MY *MIGHT!*

--FOR OF ALL THE HUMANS ON EARTH, ONLY *I* HAVE THE POWER TO DEFEAT THEM!

MILES AWAY, IN THE HEART OF NEW YORK, A TOWERING SKY-SCRAPER BECOMES EMPTY AS ITS OCCUPANTS LEAVE FOR HOME AT THE END OF A TYPICAL WORK DAY...

ONE BY ONE THE BUILDING'S LIGHTS FLICKER OUT...

...ALL EXCEPT THOSE AT THE "TOWER," THE TOWER WHICH SERVES AS HEADQUARTERS OF *THE FANTASTIC FOUR!*

AND, WITHIN THE TOWER WE FIND...

WHAT ARE YOU READING, JOHNNY?

A GREAT NEW COMIC MAG, REED! *SAY!* YOU KNOW SOMETHING--!

I'LL BE DOGGONED IF THIS MONSTER DOESN'T REMIND ME OF *THE THING!*

VER-RY FUNNY!

GIMME THAT MAG, SQUIRT! I'LL TEACH YA TO COMPARE ME TO A COMIC BOOK MONSTER!

HEY!

IF YOU WANT IT SO BAD, I'LL *WARM IT UP* FOR YOU, BIG MAN!

OWW!

COME BACK HERE!

COME 'N GET ME!

108

109

AH! THEY AGREE TO BOARD MY SHIP, AS I *PLANNED* THEY WOULD! I *KNEW* MISTER FANTASTIC COULD NOT RESIST TRYING TO LEARN WHAT MY MISSION IS!

ONE FLIP OF A SWITCH AND THEY WILL BE *MINE!*

HOLY SMOKE, REED! THIS DOCTOR DOOM CHARACTER MUST BE A REAL *WIZARD* AT INVENTING THINGS!

I *TOLD* YOU HE IS AN EVIL GENIUS! WE MUST NEVER UNDERESTIMATE HIM!

SO FAR MY PLAN IS WORKING WITHOUT A HITCH!

THEN, WITH A SUDDEN, UNEXPECTED SURGE OF ROCKET POWER THE HELICOPTER BLAZES THRU THE SKY AT ALMOST UNBELIEVABLE SPEED!

WE WILL REACH MY CASTLE STRONGHOLD WITHIN MINUTES!

AND NOW, MY *RELUCTANT* PASSENGERS, WELCOME TO THE HOME OF DOCTOR DOOM!

IT--IT'S A *REGULAR FORTRESS!*

117

118

119

120

121

122

123

THE GALE IS *FREEING* ME!! I CAN *MOVE* AGAIN! TORCH! WHERE ARE YOU??

OVER *HERE*, REED!! WE--WE'RE BEING WASHED OVERBOARD! REED!! HELP!!

SECONDS LATER, AS SUDDENLY AS IT HAD APPEARED, THE FURY OF THE STORM BLOWS ITSELF OUT TO SEA...

REED!! THING!! HELP!!

EASY, LAD! I SEE YOU! *HANG ON!*

C--CAN'T STAY AFLOAT MUCH LONGER...

GOSH, REED... I--I WAS ALMOST DONE FOR!

YOU'RE ALRIGHT NOW, TORCH! BUT WE'VE GOT TO FIND THE THING! IT'S ALMOST TIME FOR DOCTOR DOOM TO BRING US BACK!

THERE HE IS...WASHED ASHORE!

HIS DISGUISE MUST HAVE BEEN BLOWN OFF BY THE STORM!

DON'T *SAY* IT, RUBBER MAN! I KNOW! I WAS A FOOL! I MUSTA GOT CARRIED AWAY BY BEING ACCEPTED--AS A NORMAL MAN-- EVEN IF IT WAS ONLY BY A BAND OF CUT-THROAT PIRATES! I--I JUST LOST MY DUMB HEAD FOR AWHILE!

WE'RE IN LUCK, REED! HERE'S THE PIRATE CHEST! IT WAS WASHED ASHORE, ALSO!

BUT NOW, HOW IS DOCTOR DOOM GONNA GET US BACK TO THE PRESENT?

AT THAT INSTANT, ACROSS THE GULF OF CENTURIES, A HAND ACTIVATES AN ATOMIC *POWER* CIRCUIT, AND...

THEY HAVE HAD ENOUGH TIME TO OBTAIN THE GEMS OF BLACKBEARD FOR ME! AND IF THEY FAILED, THEY WILL DIE!

18

124

125

127

NOW, I'LL JUST CREATE A CIRCLE OF FLAME AROUND THE CASTLE, AND SMOKE DOCTOR DOOM OUT!!

BAH! LET HIM USE HIS FLAME! I HOPE HE BURNS MY FORTRESS TO THE GROUND, SO THAT NONE WILL EVER LEARN MY MANY SECRETS!

AS FOR ME, THE GREATEST SCIENTIFIC BRAIN OF ALL TIME IS NOT WITHOUT HIS OWN EMERGENCY ESCAPE DEVICES...SUCH AS MY ROCKET-POWERED FLYING HARNESS!

I HAVE BEEN CHEATED OUT OF THE MAGIC GEMS OF MERLIN, BUT I SHALL STILL ESCAPE...TO FIND A NEW HIDDEN SITE WHERE I CAN PLAN FOR MY CONQUEST OF EARTH!

TORCH! LOOK!

I'VE GOT TO GO AFTER HIM! MANKIND WILL NEVER BE SAFE IF DOCTOR DOOM ESCAPES!

EVEN YOUR MIRACULOUS FLAME CANNOT MATCH THE THRUST OF MY ROCKETS, TORCH!

HE'S RIGHT! I--I'M GROWING WEAK!

TOO MUCH STRAIN... CAN'T GO ON--FLAME DYING--

GOT TO KEEP ENOUGH FLAME TO BREAK MY FALL...GOT TO...

TORCH!! THAT WAS A GREAT TRY!

BAH! THEY DON'T PAY OFF FOR ALSO-RANS!

GOSH, FIRST SUB-MARINER, AND NOW DOCTOR DOOM LOOSE ON EARTH! WHAT HAPPENS NEXT?!

WE'LL DEVOTE OUR LIVES TO TRACKING THEM DOWN! WE CAN DO NO MORE!

AND NEXT TIME I'LL HANDLE THINGS MY WAY!

THE END

SURPRISE FOLLOWS SURPRISE IN THE NEXT FABULOUS ISSUE OF THE FANTASTIC FOUR!!

130

IT'S KINDA HARD TO MAKE UP YOUR MIND! YOU SEE THESE STRANGE THINGS...HEAR ALL THOSE INCREDIBLE STORIES...

IT'S MASS HYSTERIA, PETE! I COULD NO MORE BELIEVE IN THE FANTASTIC FOUR THAN I COULD IN FLYING SAUCERS!

THE HUMAN TORCH... THE THING... MISTER FANTASTIC... THE INVISIBLE GIRL...THEY'RE ALL CREATURES OF THE IMAGI---- HEY! WHA---?

HARRY... SOMETHING PUSHED US OFF OUR FEET... SOMETHING THAT BRUSHED BY US... SOMETHING ...WE CAN'T SEE!

PARDON ME, GENTLEMEN... I MUST GET BY...

A VOICE ...OUT OF THE THIN AIR!...A GIRL'S VOICE!

LOOK!... MATERIALIZING BEFORE OUR VERY EYES...

---THE INVISIBLE GIRL!

SHE'S ONE OF THE FANTASTIC FOUR! IMAGINE HER BEING AMONG US ALL THIS TIME... WITHOUT OUR KNOWING IT!

IT'S ENOUGH TO GIVE ONE THE SHIVERS!

FIRST THE HUMAN TORCH...AND NOW HER! SOMETHING'S UP FOR SURE!

DISTURBED BY THE UNCERTAIN MOOD OF THE CROWD, THE DISTAFF MEMBER OF THE FANTASTIC FOUR HASTENS TO THE GREAT SKYSCRAPER WHICH HOUSES THEIR HEADQUARTERS!

THE TORCH HAS BEEN SCOUTING FOR SIGNS OF DOCTOR DOOM! WONDER IF HE'S BROUGHT BACK ANY NEWS?

BAXTER BUILDING

IN A REMOTE CORNER OF THE BUSTLING LOBBY...

THIS EXPRESS ELEVATOR SEEMS TO BE WORKING... BUT NOT FOR ME! I'LL NEVER GET TO DELIVER MY TELEGRAM!

ARE YOU DELIVERING ANY MESSAGES TO THE FANTASTIC FOUR, SON?

ER... NO, MA'AM... (GULP)

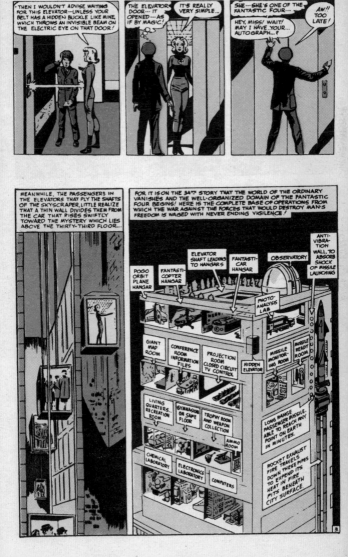

"THEN I WOULDN'T ADVISE WAITING FOR THIS ELEVATOR---UNLESS YOUR BELT HAS A HIDDEN BUCKLE LIKE MINE, WHICH THROWS AN INVISIBLE BEAM ON THE ELECTRIC EYE ON THAT DOOR!"

THE ELEVATOR DOOR... IT OPENED... AS IF BY MAGIC!

IT'S REALLY VERY SIMPLE...

SHE...SHE'S ONE OF THE FANTASTIC FOUR---

HEY, MISS! WAIT! MAY I HAVE YOUR... AUTOGRAPH...?

AW!! TOO LATE!

MEANWHILE, THE PASSENGERS IN THE ELEVATORS THAT PLY THE SHAFTS OF THE SKYSCRAPER, LITTLE REALIZE THAT A THIN WALL DIVIDES THEM FROM THE CAR THAT RISES SWIFTLY TOWARD THE MYSTERY WHICH LIES ABOVE THE THIRTY-THIRD FLOOR...

FOR IT IS ON THE 34TH STORY THAT THE WORLD OF THE ORDINARY VANISHES AND THE WELL-ORGANIZED DOMAIN OF THE FANTASTIC FOUR BEGINS! HERE IS THE COMPLETE BASE OF OPERATIONS FROM WHICH THE WAR AGAINST MAN'S FREEDOM IS WAGED WITH NEVER ENDING VIGILENCE!

POGO ORBIT PLANE HANGAR

FANTASTI-COPTER HANGAR

ELEVATOR SHAFT LEADING TO HANGARS

FANTASTI-CAR HANGAR

OBSERVATORY

ANTI-VIBRATION WALL, TO ABSORB SHOCK OF MISSILE LAUNCHING

PHOTO-ANALYSIS LAB

GIANT MAP ROOM

CONFERENCE ROOM INFORMATION FILES

PROJECTION ROOM CLOSED CIRCUIT TV CONTROL

HIDDEN ELEVATOR

MISSILE MONITOR-ING ROOM

MISSILE READY ROOM

LIVING QUARTERS, RECREATION ROOM

GYMNASIUM ON SAME FLOOR

TROPHY ROOM AND WEAPON COLLECTION

AMMO ROOM

LONG RANGE PASSENGER MISSILE, ABLE TO REACH ANY POINT ON EARTH IN MINUTES.

CHEMICAL LABORATORY

ELECTRONICS LABORATORY

COMPUTERS

ROCKET EXHAUST FIRE TRAVELS DOWN THESE PIPES TO EXPEND ITS HEAT IN FIRE PITS BENEATH CITY SURFACE

3.

133

THE INVISIBLE GIRL FINALLY EMERGES IN THE RECREATION ROOM.

TORCH! I WAS IN THE CROWD THAT WAS WATCHING YOUR RETURN... HAVE YOU...!

NOTHING TO REPORT ON DOCTOR DOOM! HE SURE KNOWS HOW TO COVER HIS TRACKS!

SURE! WHO COULDN'T HIDE FROM A HOT-HEADED TEEN-AGER? I'LL BET I COULD FIND HIM!

UNTIL WE KNOW WHAT DOCTOR DOOM IS UP TO, NONE OF US CAN FEEL SAFE!

DON'T WORRY, SIS! WHATEVER HE DOES WE'LL BE READY FOR 'IM!

IN THE MEANTIME WE HAVE A LOT OF MAIL TO CATCH UP WITH! HERE'S ANOTHER LETTER FROM THAT LITTLE BOY WHO'S HOSPITALIZED...

IN FACT HE'S AT HARMON GENERAL HOSPITAL, RIGHT ACROSS THE STREET! THIS LETTER GIVES HIS FLOOR AND THE LOCATION OF HIS ROOM! SAY...

...WON'T HE BE TICKLED IF I JUST DROP IN FOR A VISIT, UNEXPECTEDLY! IT'LL SURE GIVE HIM SOMETHING TO TALK ABOUT WITH HIS FELLOW "SHUT-INS!"

WHA--? I-I MUST BE SEEING THINGS! B-BUT NO! IT... IT'S MISTER FANTASTIC... IN PERSON!

I THOUGHT YOU MIGHT LIKE A CHAT, TOMMY!

HAPPILY, THE YOUNGSTER BUBBLES OVER, THROWING MANY QUESTIONS AT HIS FAMOUS GUEST!

WELL...THE REASON MY COSTUME STRETCHES TO ANY LENGTH THAT I DO, IS THAT IT IS WOVEN FROM CHEMICAL FIBERS CONTAINING UNSTABLE MOLECULES THAT SHIFT IN STRUCTURE WHEN I AFFECT THE CHANGE!

BUT THE GENERAL PUBLIC IS MADE UP OF CRITICS AS WELL AS FRIENDS... AND THERE ARE CHALLENGES AS WELL AS QUESTIONS!

"...AND IF THE THING WILL MEET US ON THE CORNER OF ASHBY AND MAIN STREET, WE'LL KNOCK THAT CHIP OFF HIS SHOULDER AND MAKE HIM LIKE IT!
SIGNED--"

"...THE YANCY STREET GANG!" I'VE HEARD FROM THOSE MEALY-MOUTHED BRAGGARTS BEFORE! THEY GET THEIR KICKS OUT OF TRYIN' TO RILE ME!

WELL, ARE YOU GONNA ANSWER THEM, THING?

YOU *BET* I WILL!--THIS BLOCK IS TITANIUM STEEL--6 INCHES THICK AND THE STRONGEST METAL KNOWN TO MAN!

I'LL JUST ROLL IT BY HAND INTO A FORM ACCEPTABLE FOR MAILING---I WOULDN'T WANT THE YANCY GANG TO THINK I WASN'T NEAT--

GASP.

HERE! SEND THIS TO THEM! AND ON THE DAY THEY MANAGE TO UNROLL IT, I'LL PERSONALLY CONGRATULATE 'EM!

WHEW!

BAH! IF ONLY I COULD FACE AN ENEMY WORTHY OF MY STRENGTH! A FOE LIKE DOCTOR DOOM... OR SUB-MARINER!

I'LL PICK DOCTOR DOOM FOR OUTRIGHT VILLAINY! SUB-MARINER IS HOSTILE BECAUSE HE'S HURT AND BITTER!

WHAT'S THE DIFFERENCE? IF THERE'S AN ILL-WIND BLOWING ANYWHERE, ONE OF THOSE TWO HAS PROBABLY STARTED IT!

YES, AN *ILL-WIND IS BLOWING!* IT IS NOT YET A CYCLONE, NOR EVEN A HARSH GUST... *AS YET,* IT IS A GENTLE *ZEPHYR* TOUCHING THE PLACID WATERS OF THE OCEAN, FROM WHICH PLAYFUL PORPOISE LEAP AT THE BLUE SKY!

LOOK! THERE'S A WHOLE SCHOOL OF PORPOISE KEEPING PACE WITH THE SHIP!

WHAT A LOVELY SIGHT! THEY'RE LIKE CHILDREN AT PLAY!

CHILDREN! IF THE SUNLIGHT WASN'T KNOWN TO PLAY TRICKS WITH ONE'S VISION, I'D SWEAR THAT WAS A *MAN* AMONG THOSE PORPOISES!

NOW, MY SUBJECTS... THE NEXT MANEUVER...

ALAS, IT IS ONE OF THOSE TIMES WHEN VISION IS ACCURATE BUT WHO COULD BELIEVE THE MOST AMAZING OF SIGHTS--PRINCE NAMOR-- KNOWN TO ALL MORTALS AS--*SUBMARINER!*

EXCELLENT! WELL DONE!

MEANWHILE, HIGH ABOVE THE SCENE OF INNOCENT FROLIC, AN EVIL PRESENCE HOVERS... SEARCHING THE BROAD EXPANSE OF WATER WITH A BALEFUL, ELECTRONIC EYE...

AH! I'VE FINALLY FOUND HIM! I KNEW MY TELEVISION SCANNER WOULD PICK HIM UP AT LOW LEVEL FOCUS! NOW, SUBMARINER ---WE HAVE WORK TO DO!

I'LL BUZZ HIM AT WAVE HEIGHT! THAT'LL ATTRACT HIS ATTENTION!

WELL! WELL! SO A SURFACE MORTAL DARES INVADE THE PRIVACY OF PRINCE NAMOR!

SUBMARINER'S VANISHED BENEATH THE SEA! BUT THIS AEROSUB CAN TRAIL HIM THERE, TOO!

I'LL JUST SURPRISE THAT CURIOSITY SEEKER AND GIVE HIM MORE THAN HE BARGAINED FOR!

WHA..?

THIS OUGHT TO SET HIM BACK ON HIS HEELS! HMMM... HIS CRAFT IS OF STRANGE DESIGN! I WONDER WHO HE IS?

I COME IN PEACE, SUBMARINER! OUR MEETING HAS BEEN INEVITABLE, AND LONG DELAYED!

IS THAT SO? COME OUT WHERE I CAN GET A GOOD LOOK AT YOU!

SO YOU SHALL! BEHOLD THE FACE OF YOUR NEW ALLY! THE ONE WHO SHARES YOUR AMBITION --- THE PUNISHMENT AND TOTAL DEFEAT OF THE FANTASTIC FOUR... AND THEN OF ALL MANKIND!

THAT IS STRONG TALK---- WHOEVER YOU ARE!

NEVER FEAR! I AM STRONG--- STRONG ENOUGH TO JOIN THE POWERS OF SCIENCE TO THOSE OF DARKNESS! SHOW ME THE PUNY MORTAL WHO DOES NOT TREMBLE AT THE NAME OF DOCTOR DOOM!

FANTASTIC FOUR in Stan Lee + J. KIRBY
"WHEN SUPER-MENACES UNITE"

PART 2

EAGER FOR A PARLEY, DOCTOR DOOM FOLDS BACK THE WINGS OF HIS AERO SUB AND NOSES IT INTO THE DEPTHS OF THE SEA, AS SUBMARINER DARTS THROUGH THE COLD GREEN SHADOWS OF HIS DOMAIN!

THEY MOVE ACROSS SUBMERGED CANYONS AND VALLEYS, OVER THE RUINS OF A ONCE PROUD CITY WHERE A VANISHED RACE ONCE LIVED IN HARMONY--GHOST VOICES THAT ONCE HAILED SUBMARINER AS PRINCE NAMOR!

SUBMARINER FINALLY LEADS DOCTOR DOOM TO HIS NEW QUARTERS, A LARGE, DOMED VILLA IN A FIELD OF SWAYING UNDERSEA VEGETATION! THE AIRLOCK OPENS TO ADMIT THEM...

137

RELAXING AMID THE COMFORT OF SUBMARINER'S NEW HOME, DOCTOR DOOM REVEALS HIS THOUGHTS!

IT WOULD APPEAR THAT YOU'VE TAKEN A HOLIDAY FROM YOUR CAMPAIGN AGAINST THE SURFACE WORLD! MEN NO LONGER SPEAK YOUR NAME IN FEAR!

THEN THEY ARE FOOLS! MY WRATH CAN EASILY REAWAKEN THEIR FEARS!

AHHH! THE INVISIBLE GIRL! SO SHE'S THE REASON FOR YOUR CHANGED ATTITUDE! OF COURSE! IF YOU WAGE WAR AGAINST THE FANTASTIC FOUR...YOU MUST BE HER ENEMY, TOO!

TAKE CARE! THAT FEMALE IS NO CONCERN OF YOURS!

I'M MAKING IT MY CONCERN, SUBMARINER! IT MUST BE EVIDENT BY THIS TIME THAT TO DEFEAT THE FANTASTIC FOUR... IT MAY TAKE A "DIABOLICAL DUO"... YOU AND I ... STRIKING OUT FOR POWER AND REVENGE!

"WHAT HAS HAPPENED TO YOUR THIRST FOR REVENGE? HAVE YOU FORGOTTEN THE GLISTENING TOWERS OF YOUR ONCE-GREAT CIVILIZATION--- THE CULTURE AND COMFORT ENJOYED BY YOUR HAPPY SUBJECTS!"

"WHERE ARE YOUR PEOPLE AND THEIR PROUD WORKS? IMAGINE HOW THEY HAD TO FLEE FOR THEIR LIVES BEFORE THE BARBARIANS FROM THE SURFACE COULD CONDUCT THEIR UNDERWATER H-BOMB TEST IN THIS PARTICULAR AREA..."

"FORTUNATELY, YOU WERE ABSENT DURING THE DESTRUCTION... BUT THE RUINS TESTIFY TO WHAT MUST HAVE HAPPENED! AND YOUR VANISHED SUBJECTS--- WILL YOU EVER AGAIN FIND THEM AS YOU SEARCH THE ENDLESS DEPTHS?"

IMAGINE-- YOUR GREAT AND PROUD PEOPLE-- STRUGGLING FOR THOUSANDS OF YEARS, DEFEATING ALL THE TERRORS OF THE DEEP TO BUILD A CIVILIZATION SUPERB AND BEAUTIFUL... YES, BEAUTIFUL AND GLOWING WITH LIFE... UNTIL THAT LAST TERRIFYING MOMENT... WHEN THAT MONSTER OF A BOMB LODGED IN THE MIDST OF THAT BEAUTY...

GONE! ALL THAT GLORIOUS HISTORY GONE IN ONE BRIEF INSTANT!... REPLACED BY AN UGLY CRATER IN THE OCEAN FLOOR...LITTERED WITH FUSED MASONRY AND BITTER MEMORIES THAT CRY OUT... *REVENGE! REVENGE!!*

REVENGE UPON THE SURFACE WORLD WHICH DID THIS IN ITS IGNORANCE! REVENGE UPON HUMANITY'S DEFENDERS! DEATH TO THE FANTASTIC FOUR!

I...I...I CANNOT HARM THE GIRL! BUT I WILL AID YOU IN DEFEATING THE OTHERS!

VERY WELL THEN! I AGREE! BUT BEFORE I TELL YOU OF MY PLAN, LET ME DEMONSTRATE THE POWER OF MY MAGNETIC BRAINCHILDREN!

I CALL THIS CYLINDER A "GRABBER"! AT A TOUCH OF THIS CONTROL KNOB, I CAN LAUNCH IT IN ANY DIRECTION! OBSERVE!

TRAVELING ON ITS MAGNETIC BEAM, THE GRABBER SWIFTLY, TIRELESSLY COVERS VAST DISTANCES OF THE UNDERSEA KINGDOM...

AS IF IT HAD A WILL OF ITS OWN, THE GRABBER ZEROES IN ON THE HEAD OF A HUGE PAGAN IDOL, MIRED FOR CENTURIES IN THE OOZE OF THE SEA BOTTOM...

THE HUGE MASS BEGINS TO STIR, TREMBLING IN THE PULL OF A TITANIC, UNSEEN FORCE! SLOWLY, IT IS LIFTED FROM THE STRONG GRIP OF ITS AGE OLD PRISON...

THEN, WITH ONE SUDDEN, FRIGHTFUL YANK, THE MAMMOTH IDOL'S HEAD BREAKS FREE AND DRIFTS LIKE A FEATHER ON THE MAGNETIC CURRENT TRAVELLED BY THE GRABBER!

139

FINALLY...

THERE! WHEN I RELEASE THIS KNOB, MY GRABBER BRINGS BACK ITS CATCH... NO MATTER HOW HEAVY, OR HOW LARGE.

SOME CATCH! THAT IDOL'S HEAD MUST WEIGH COUNTLESS TONS! YOU MEAN THAT LITTLE CYLINDER WAS ABLE TO LIFT ALL *THAT?*

MAGNETIC FORCE IS UNLIMITED! AND WHEN AMPLIFIED, IT HAS THE STRENGTH OF GIANTS! ALL THAT POWER IS LOCKED IN THIS SMALL CYLINDER!

NOW I SHALL DISMANTLE THE GRABBER! YOU WILL BE ABLE TO HIDE ITS TINY PARTS IN THE HOLLOW OF YOUR BELT BUCKLE!

DONE! I TAKE IT THAT I AM TO REASSEMBLE THE GRABBER AT SOME POINT IN YOUR PLAN... WHEN YOU'RE READY TO RELEASE ITS INCREDIBLE POWER!

YES... WHEN YOU COME FACE TO FACE WITH OUR ENEMIES... THE FANTASTIC FOUR! NOW LISTEN CLOSELY.

SOON AFTER-- ABOVE THE OCEAN'S SURFACE...

LOOK! BELOW US... SOMETHING'S BEEN SHOT OUT OF THE WATER!

HOLY HANNAH! CHECK OUR COURSE! WE MAY HAVE DRIFTED INTO AN AREA WHERE OUR SUBS ARE TESTING POLARIS MISSILES!

YEEOWWW!! THE MISSILE'S COMING RIGHT FOR US!

NO TIME TO DODGE! IT'S GOING TO HIT HEAD ON!

WAIT! THAT'S NOT A *MISSILE!* IT'S...

BAH! THAT'S ENOUGH HORSEPLAY! I MUSTN'T FORGET MY MISSION!

TELL ME WHAT WE SAW WASN'T TRUE! IT *COULDN'T* HAVE BEEN REAL!

I'M SURE NOT GONNA WRITE IT IN OUR LOG BOOK! NOBODY WOULD BELIEVE US!

10

SUBMARINER WASTES LITTLE TIME! HE BECOMES A METEOR, A LIGHTNING BOLT, A STREAK ACROSS THE MIDDAY SKY...SPEEDING TOWARD THE COASTLINE OF AMERICA!

THAT FERRYBOAT WILL MAKE A GREAT SNAPSHOT, MATILDA! JUST THE KIND OF MEMENTO TO REMIND US OF OUR VISIT TO THE BIG CITY!

HIRAM...!

A MOMENT LATER... IN THE CITY ITSELF...

WHAT'S ALL THAT COMMOTION?

WOW! LOOK WHO'S COMING UP THE STREET!

OH, MY!

FEARLESS, CALM--- FULLY AWARE OF HIS GREAT POWERS, SUBMARINER CONFIDENTLY MAKES HIS WAY THROUGH THE UNEASY, STARING CROWDS...

NO FOOLIN'! IT'S SUBMARINER, I TELL YA! HE LOOKS JUST LIKE HE DOES IN THE STORIES I'VE READ!

WHY IS HE HERE? WHAT IS HE UP TO?

HE DON'T LOOK SO TOUGH TO ME!

STAND ASIDE! I FROWN UPON ANY INTERFERENCE FROM MERE MORTALS!

GET HIM! HE ACTS LIKE HE OWNS THE TOWN!

THE FANTASTIC FOUR WILL TAKE HIM DOWN A PEG! JUST WAIT'LL THEY FIND OUT HE'S HERE!

SAY! DO YOU THINK HE'S COME FOR A SHOWDOWN!

SUBMARINER IGNORES THE VARIED EMOTIONS HE STIRS AMONG THE POPULACE... EVEN THE APPEARANCE OF THE POLICE DISTURBS HIM LITTLE AS HE CONTINUES ON HIS WAY...

IT'S SUBMARINER! WE CAN TURN HIM IN FOR CREATING A DISTURBANCE!

EASY! DON'T BORROW TROUBLE BEFORE IT STARTS! WE'LL ALERT THE ENTIRE FORCE-- IN CASE WE HAVE TO TAKE HIM!

BUT THE TENSION, EVER PRESENT DURING THE RARE APPEARANCES OF THE SEA LORD, SEEMS TO BLANKET THE CITY--- IT SEEPS INTO CORNERS AND CREVICES, REACHING EVERYWHERE... EVEN INTO THE HEAD- QUARTERS OF THE FANTASTIC FOUR.

HEY! WHAT'S GLISTENING BEHIND THIS SHELF OF BOOKS?

11.

WAIT..!! PRINCE NAMOR FEARS NOTHING ON THIS PLANET! LET HIM DO HIS WORST!

WE'LL SEE HOW BRAVE YOU ARE, MISTER BIG TALK! I THINK I'LL SOFTEN-UP YOUR STEEL NERVES BEFORE I REALLY GO TO WORK ON YOU!

THE HUMAN TORCH BURNS A CIRCLE OF FIRE INTO THE FLOOR AROUND SUBMARINER! AND WHEN IT'S COMPLETED...

JUST THE KIND OF CHILDISH PRANK I'D EXPECT FROM YOU!

YOU WON'T THINK SO IN ONE SECOND!!

SUDDENLY, THE FLOOR GIVES WAY BENEATH SUBMARINER'S FEET AS THE FLAMING CIRCLE FALLS INTO THE ROOM BELOW!

WELL, YOU CAN SEE I DID NOT FALL THROUGH! YOU FORGOT I HAVE THE POWER TO DEFY GRAVITY!

BUT, UNLIKE YOU, MY POWER DOES NOT FADE, EVEN AS YOUR FLAME BEGINS TO FADE NOW!

AND INDEED, BEFORE THE HUMAN TORCH CAN ACT, HIS WHITE HOT FLAME LOSES ITS CONSISTENCY AND BEGINS TO COOL ---UNTIL ---

MY FLAME HAS RUN ITS TIME LIMIT! I'M CHANGING BACK TO HUMAN FORM! I'VE FAILED! ...FAILED!

FATE HAS GIVEN YOU A REPRIEVE, SUBMARINER! ...NOW SPEAK... OR GIVE BATTLE!

I'VE COME TO SEEK YOUR TRUST! YOU SEE, MINE IS A LONELY KINGDOM...AND A LASTING FRIENDSHIP MAY PROVE OF MORE VALUE THAN ANY FLEETING TASTE OF REVENGE!!

VERY IMPRESSIVE, SUBMARINER! ONLY I'M NOT INCLINED TO SHAKE YOUR HAND TOO READILY! HOW DO WE KNOW IT'S NOT A PLOT? HOW DO WE KNOW YOU HAVEN'T SET A TRAP?

YEAH! YOU'D BETTER DO SOME FAST CHECKING, PAL! I'LL KEEP AN EYE ON HIM!

OH, PLEASE LISTEN TO HIM! CAN'T YOU SEE HE'S SINCERE?

I'M STILL FOR CHECKING! COME ON, 'TORCH! WE CAN LOOK IN ON EVERY ROOM BY CLOSED CIRCUIT TELEVISION!

WE CAN FIND OUT SOON ENOUGH IF HE'S SET ANY TRAPS IN HERE!

144

LOBBY   MISSILE LAUNCH AREA   CONFERENCE ROOM   MA

CHEMISTRY LAB   ELECTRONICS LAB   MAP STUDY   PHO

PROJECTION ROOM... ALL CLEAR!

ROOF LANDING STRIP... RIGHT CORNER --- ALL CLEAR!

OBSERVATORY

I DON'T GET IT! WE'VE SCANNED EVERY CORNER OF OUR BASE OF OPERATIONS WITHOUT FINDING ONE BOOBY TRAP! NOTHING SEEMS AMISS! YET, I CAN'T GET RID OF THE FEELING THAT SUBMARINER'S BEEN UP TO NO GOOD!

LUCKILY THE WORKING DAY IS OVER! THE REST OF THE BUILDING IS EMPTY! WE CAN CHECK THAT OUT TOO!

WELL, MY SUSPICIOUS FRIEND-- DOES MY PRESENCE HERE PASS YOUR RIGID INSPECTION!

I'M NOT SATISFIED YET, SUBMARINER! STAY WHERE YOU ARE! I'M COMING BACK TO ASK A FEW MORE QUESTIONS!

WELL, YOU'LL JUST HAVE TO WAIT FOR THE TIME BEING! I'M ON A HOLIDAY--- AND I'VE DECIDED TO TAKE THIS CHARMING YOUNG LADY ON A TOUR OF THE CITY..

LIBRARY

SUBMARINER'S FLIPPANT MOOD SUDDENLY VANISHES AS A LOUD TREMOR SHAKES THE ENTIRE BUILDING!

CRACK

SLOWLY, SMOOTHLY THE GREAT SKYSCRAPER BEGINS TO RISE FREE OF ITS FOUNDATION... BEGINS TO RISE ABOVE THE NOW-DESERTED STREETS....

THE BUILDING... IT'S RISING INTO THE AIR!

WE'RE GOING HIGHER-- FASTER--

THIS IS YOUR DOING, SUBMARINER! YOU CAN STOP THIS!

I CAN'T, YOU FOOLS! I PLANTED THE TRAP... BUT IT'S BEEN TRIGGERED BY DOCTOR DOOM!

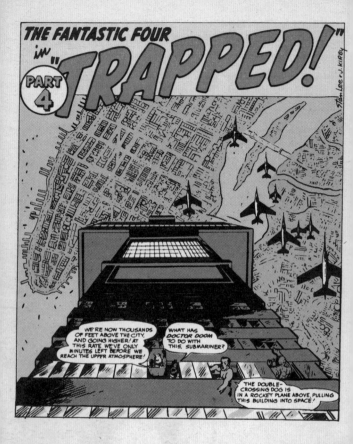

147

148

149

150

151

152

AND HERE'S THE REST OF IT... *FULL BLAST!* YOU DIDN'T KILL ME WITH THAT ELECTRIC CHARGE! LIKE AN ELECTRIC EEL, I ABSORBED IT, STORED IT, AND NOW...I'M *RETURNING* IT!

A-AAAAA-AA...GOT TO GET OUT OF HERE BEFORE I...

DOCTOR DOOM FLINGS OPEN A FLOOR ESCAPE HATCH! THE OUTRUSHING AIR LITERALLY EXPLODES HIM AWAY FROM THE SHIP...INTO THE VAST, COLD REACHES OF SPACE!

HIS HIGH RATE OF SPEED CARRIES HIM INTO THE COURSE TAKEN BY THE METEOR SWARM! INSTINCTIVELY, HE REACHES OUT FOR SUPPORT AND FRANTICALLY CLUTCHES A SPEEDING METEOR!

THE ROCKY SPACE WANDERER STREAKS ONWARD, UNMINDFUL OF ITS HUMAN RIDER...UNMINDFUL OF THE LONLINESS OF ITS NEVER-ENDING JOURNEY...

FOR ETERNITY IS A LONG, LONG TIME, AND DOCTOR DOOM, WHO HAS COVETED ALL OF THE EARTH, NOW HAS ALL OF ETERNITY TO SCHEME IN A MUCH LARGER DOMAIN! THE UNIVERSE ITSELF!

WHILE, BACK ON EARTH, THE HOUR IS LATE... THE DARK STREETS DESERTED ON SKYSCRAPER ROW... AND THE STRAY INDIVIDUALS WHO LATER WITNESS THE SILENT RETURN OF THE BAXTER BUILDING FROM THE SKIES, WRITE IT OFF AS A BAD DREAM...AN HALLUCINATION RESULTING FROM THE ANXIETIES THAT PLAGUE OUR NUCLEAR SOCIETY...

BUT, TO THE FANTASTIC FOUR, THE SIGHT OF THE CITY IS A MIRACLE GREATER THAN THEIR INCREDIBLE EXPERIENCE!

WE'RE HOME! HOME!

THE SUBMARINER, IN DOCTOR DOOM'S SPACE SHIP, HAS GUIDED THE BUILDING BACK TO ITS FOUNDATION! THANKS TO HIM WE'RE ALIVE!

154

Four human beings--changed by space-born cosmic rays into something more than merely human.

So was born The Fantastic Four-- and from that moment on, the world would never again be the same.

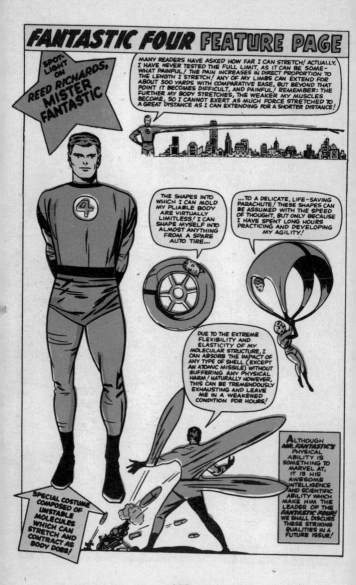

FANTASTIC FOUR FEATURE PAGE

SPOT-LIGHT ON Reed Richards, MISTER FANTASTIC

MANY READERS HAVE ASKED HOW FAR I CAN STRETCH! ACTUALLY, I HAVE NEVER TESTED THE FULL LIMIT, AS IT CAN BE SOMEWHAT PAINFUL! THE PAIN INCREASES IN DIRECT PROPORTION TO THE LENGTH I STRETCH! ANY OF MY LIMBS CAN EXTEND FOR ABOUT 500 YARDS WITH COMPARATIVE EASE, BUT BEYOND THAT POINT IT BECOMES DIFFICULT, AND PAINFUL! REMEMBER: THE FURTHER MY BODY STRETCHES, THE WEAKER MY MUSCLES BECOME, SO I CANNOT EXERT AS MUCH FORCE STRETCHED TO A GREAT DISTANCE AS I CAN EXTENDING FOR A SHORTER DISTANCE!

THE SHAPES INTO WHICH I CAN MOLD MY PLIABLE BODY ARE VIRTUALLY LIMITLESS! I CAN SHAPE MYSELF INTO ALMOST ANYTHING FROM A SPARE AUTO TIRE...

...TO A DELICATE, LIFE-SAVING PARACHUTE! THESE SHAPES CAN BE ASSUMED WITH THE SPEED OF THOUGHT, BUT ONLY BECAUSE I HAVE SPENT LONG HOURS PRACTICING AND DEVELOPING MY AGILITY!

DUE TO THE EXTREME FLEXIBILITY AND ELASTICITY OF MY MOLECULAR STRUCTURE, I CAN ABSORB THE IMPACT OF ANY TYPE OF SHELL (EXCEPT AN ATOMIC MISSILE) WITHOUT SUFFERING ANY PHYSICAL HARM! NATURALLY HOWEVER, THIS CAN BE TREMENDOUSLY EXHAUSTING AND LEAVE ME IN A WEAKENED CONDITION FOR HOURS!

ALTHOUGH MR. FANTASTIC'S PHYSICAL ABILITY IS SOMETHING TO MARVEL AT, IT IS HIS AWESOME INTELLIGENCE AND SCIENTIFIC ABILITY WHICH MAKE HIM THE LEADER OF THE FANTASTIC FOUR! WE SHALL DISCUSS THESE STRIKING QUALITIES IN A FUTURE ISSUE!

SPECIAL COSTUME COMPOSED OF UNSTABLE MOLECULES WHICH CAN STRETCH AND CONTRACT AS BODY DOES!

EPILOGUE

And there you have it—the first six issues of one of the most memorable comicbook series of all time!

But do not despair, O Seeker of the Truth. What you have just finished reading in awesome wonder is but the tip of the Marvel iceberg. Many are the sagas still to unfold. Many are the wonders yet to come. Many are the subsequent volumes calculated to separate you from your last remaining shekels.

See ya in our next volume!

Stan